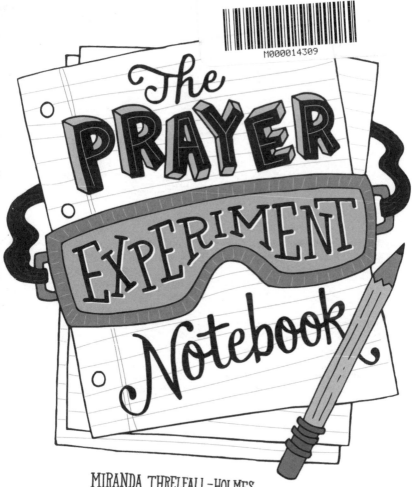

The PRAYER EXPERIMENT Notebook

MIRANDA THRELFALL-HOLMES
& MINA MUNNS

spck

For Tobias & Zoë

First published in Great Britain in 2018

Society for Promoting Christian Knowledge
36 Causton Street, London SW1P 4ST
www.spck.org.uk

Text copyright © Miranda Threlfall-Holmes and Mina Munns 2018
Illustrations copyright © Patrick Laurent

The author and publisher have made every effort to ensure that the external website and email addresses included in this book are correct and up to date at the time of going to press. The author and publisher are not responsible for the content, quality or continuing accessibility of the sites.

British Library Cataloguing-in-Publication Data
A catalogue record for this book is available from the British Library

ISBN 978-0-281-07847-9
eBook ISBN 978-0-281-07848-6

1 3 5 7 9 10 8 6 4 2

Typeset and designed by Fiona Andreanelli
Manufacture managed by Jellyfish
Printed in Great Britain by CPI

eBook by www.andreanelli.com

Produced on paper from sustainable forests

CONTENTS

BONUS SECTION: GROUP ACTIVITIES

ABOUT THE AUTHORS

Miranda is the Team Rector of the St Luke in the City team of churches in Liverpool. After first working as a brand manager and a historian, she trained for ministry at Cranmer Hall, Durham, and has worked in parishes in Newcastle and Durham and as a university chaplain. Her publications include

The Essential History of Christianity (SPCK, 2012) and *Being a Chaplain* (SPCK, 2011) as well as the other books in the Prayer Experiment series, *The Teenage Prayer Experiment Notebook* (written with her teenage son Noah, SPCK, 2015) and *The Little Book of Prayer Experiments* (SPCK, 2016).

Mina is a curate of St Helen's, Selston, and St Mary's, Westwood, in the Diocese of Southwell and Nottingham. She is a former primary school teacher and church children's worker and, like Miranda, trained for ministry at Cranmer Hall. Mina writes the craft page for *Premier Youth and Children's Work* magazine and, in addition to blogging at Flame Creative Children's Ministry,

writes 'The Well: Creative Children's Ministry' blog
for children's leaders in the Methodist Church.

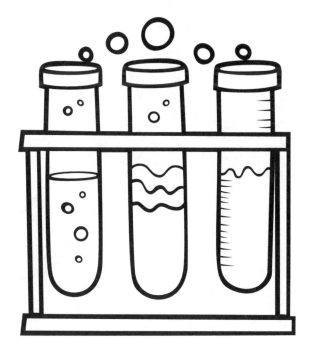

ACKNOWLEDGEMENTS

This book has developed from two different starting points. Mina has been running the Flame Creative Children's Ministry website of Christian resources for children's spirituality (<www.flamecreativekids. blogspot.co.uk>) for the last five years and has a special interest in helping children to connect with God in creative ways. Flame has had over three million page-views and in 2014 was the runner-up in the 'Most inspiring leadership blog' category at the Premier Christian Radio New Media Awards.

Miranda and her teenage son began experimenting with different methods of prayer as a blog, 'The Teenage Prayer Experiment', in which Miranda wrote an idea for prayer each week, and then her son Noah tried it out and blogged about how he had found it. As the blog got more popular, the ideas began to be used by individuals and church youth groups around the country, and were published by SPCK as *The Teenage Prayer Experiment Notebook* in 2015. By popular demand, a version for adults — *The Little Book of Prayer Experiments* — was published the following year. This book is the result of requests for a version for younger children, primarily in the 8-12 age group.

We would particularly like to thank the following for experimenting, for sharing their feedback with us and with you, and for being so open, honest and thoughtful in describing how it was for them: Alex Greenwood, Daniel Rix, Emma Arnold, Grace Munns, Joss Lawrence, Lucy Lucas, Marco Lucas, Phoebe Wakefield, Poppy Lawrence, Solomon Lawrence, Tara Harper, Tobias Threlfall-Holmes and Zoë Threlfall-Holmes.

HOW TO USE
THIS BOOK

his is not a book about prayer by
experts. It is a book of experiments
in prayer for you to try for yourself.
It includes space for you to make notes on
how you found each one, and notes from other
experimenters so that you can compare your
experiences and reactions with those of other
children who have tried them out.

There will be experiments that you like, and probably ones that you don't like too. You can only know which are which by trying them out. You'll see from the other experimenters' notes that different people like different things, and some have also made suggestions for improvements or variations to the experiments.

You don't have to read this book from front to back, or try the experiments in any particular order, or even try all the experiments. We have put them in this order so that different styles of prayer are mixed up. But you can choose to do them in any order, or just pick out the ones that sound most interesting.

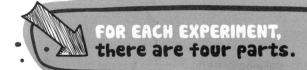

FOR EACH EXPERIMENT,
there are four parts.

1 A brief introduction to the prayer idea
  being suggested.

2 The experiment itself: what to do and any
  equipment you will need.

3 Space for your own notes on what using
  that prayer idea was like: what happened,
  how did it make you feel, would you do
  anything differently if you were repeating
  the experiment?

4 Reviews from other experimenters, so you
  can compare your experience with theirs.

It is up to you whether or not you read the other experimenters' notes before doing the experiment yourself. You may find that reading their notes helps you to identify the experiments that appeal to you the most. Or you may prefer to try the experiments without being influenced by what anyone else thought, then compare notes later.

The most important thing is that you actually try the experiments out! We have both found that the only way to tell what praying in a particular way is like is to try it. It is no good just reading about it. So even if you want to read this book through before starting, do then choose one experiment, put the book down and give it a try.

We hope you enjoy experimenting!

Miranda & Mina

PLAY
DOUGH
PRAYERS

PLAY DOUGH PRAYERS

The most common form of prayer is asking God to help people. When we are worried about someone we can ask God to look after them. When something worries us — maybe a situation we have heard about or something at school or home — we can ask God to change what is happening and help the people who are affected to cope.

You may have heard people talk about 'intercessions'. These are a type of prayer that involve praying not just for ourselves but also for other people and other places. We are 'interceding' or being a 'go-between' for those people, asking God to help them.

These play dough prayers are intercessions, helping you to pray for others by using your hands and making shapes. Sometimes people talk about prayer in terms of 'holding things before God' or 'giving things to God'. By making a simple model of the thing you are praying for, you can really imagine holding it up before God and asking God to look after it. Then you can squish it up and make the next thing. You don't need to keep each model, because you have handed those concerns over to God.

THE EXPERIMENT

Have a go at these ideas for play dough shapes, but feel free to make your own shapes and pray for other things that are worrying you or people you know, using whatever shape reminds you of them.

 YOU WILL NEED: A lump of play dough.

1 Make the play dough into a ball. Pray for the world. Thank God for creation

and all the things he has made in the world. Pray for places where there is war and famine. Pray for people who care for the world.

2 Make the play dough into a cross. Pray for the Church. Pray for Christians who are put into prison because they believe in Jesus. Pray for people who lead the Church. Pray for your own church and the people you know there. Pray that people who don't know who Jesus is will come to know him.

3 Make the play dough into a heart. Pray for
people. Pray for your family and friends.
Pray for people who have no family and
friends or have nowhere to live. Pray for
people who are ill and lonely. Pray that God
will help you to bless people.

4 Make the play dough into the initial letter of your name. Pray for yourself. Ask God to bless you and to help you with the things you are finding hard at the moment. Ask God to help you to help others. Thank God for the good things he has given you.

MY NOTES

When I tried this...

Things I found most helpful were...

Things I might do differently next time were...

Marks out of 10:

WHAT OTHER EXPERIMENTERS THOUGHT

Poppy (11) I enjoyed being able to mould the play dough into things I was praying for. I really liked making the world because I actually used a pencil and drew out the countries and then I prayed for all of the different countries. 8/10

Zoë (8) This was fun — who doesn't like play dough? It felt different because I was playing. I did pray for the four things, but then in the middle of each one I'd forget and just start playing with the play dough. But when I remembered I was meant to be praying it did then help me pray for fun things and thank God for toys and playing. But I did find it hard to concentrate because I kept getting distracted. 3/10

Alex (11) I didn't like it because it was very hard to put together and make the shapes and if you were to try to hold them they would just break. 1/10

Joss (9) I liked this one. My brother said, 'You looked like you were focused.' When I was making the ball to represent the Earth it reminded me of all the refugees and all the wealthy people who could have saved all of them. 9/10

THANK YOU JAR

Saying thank you is a very important part of praying. But we don't say thank you to God for quite the same reasons that we thank other people. We don't say thank you to God just to be polite or to make God feel better! Saying thank you to God means that we are doing two important things.

First, we are choosing to concentrate on being grateful for the good things in life. There is an old saying, 'Count your blessings', and it is generally true that if we focus on the good things in life rather than the bad, we are likely to be much happier. Focusing on the positive doesn't mean ignoring the bad things in life — after all, sometimes things are seriously wrong and need to be changed. But even in some of the worst situations there are likely to be some good things that we can give thanks to God for.

Second, when we thank God for all the good things we have received, we are acknowledging that everything comes from God. This means that we recognize God as the Creator, the basic source of everything, from the Big Bang onwards. It also means recognizing that all the good things we have are not ours by right, but are gifts. This helps us to develop a healthy sense of ourselves — we are special and loved by God and, at the same time, we are no more special than anyone else.

Because it means all this, saying thank you
to God is an important part of the Christian
tradition of prayer, but it can become quite
repetitive and boring. We often find that when
it comes to
saying thank
you, our minds
go blank! Or we
repeat ourselves,
saying thank you to
God for the same,
obvious things
every time we
pray.

THE EXPERIMENT

Try making a thank you jar as a way to collect together everything you want to say thank you to God for, and use it as a resource for prayer.

YOU WILL NEED: A jam jar and some coloured paper.

1 Get an empty, clean jam jar with the label removed, or some other pot or bowl. Cut some paper (coloured paper works well if you're using a glass jar) into strips.

2 On each piece of paper, write one thing
that you are thankful for, and add the strip
to the jar. Keep a spare supply of pieces
of paper next to the jar and whenever you
think of something new to say thanks for,
write it down and add it to the jar.

3 Keep your thank you jar somewhere safe
where you will see it regularly – perhaps
on your windowsill, bedside table or in a
prayer corner with any other prayer items
that you may have. When you sit down to
pray, take a handful of the contents out
and say thank you for those things, and add
any new ones that you have thought of that
day to the jar. Doing this will mean that you
keep some variety in your prayers and also

Slowly build up a collection of more and more things to be thankful for.

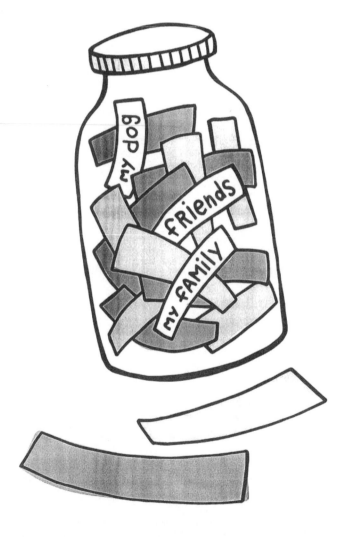

MY NOTES

When I tried this...

Things I found most helpful were...

Things I might do differently next time were...

Marks out of 10:

WHAT OTHER EXPERIMENTERS THOUGHT

Alex (11) I found it really amazing. I think this activity is one of the best activities. I found it really interesting because it made you think what you were thankful for. I became addicted to putting things in it. 8/10

Solomon (7) I liked doing this because it was a really good way to pray for things that I forgot to be thankful for. I said thank you because we are safe and have good things to entertain us. 7/10

Joss (9) It's really useful. If you're down you can go and see something to be thankful for. We had fun thinking what we were thankful for. In a strange way it was fun instead of focusing on what we didn't have. 8/10

Poppy (11) It was really fun to think of all our favourite things and things we needed so that we could pray about them. I was thankful for friends and holidays. It was fun thinking of stuff you'd normally take for granted. It was fun to think of the happy things. 8/10

Emma (11) I decorated a jar with shiny paper and wrote ten thank yous on coloured paper. I placed this on my windowsill in my bedroom. When I tried this experiment it made me feel sorry for other people who did not have what I have. It made me feel more aware of people without food or water. I liked having a written reminder of my thank yous. 9/10

PAPER
CHAIN
PRAYERS

PAPER CHAIN PRAYERS

Did you know that scientists estimate there are ten million different colours in the world? From pale yellow to dark purple and everything in between, there are so many colours, and everyone has their favourite.

Sometimes colours can make us think of different things. Red might mean 'stop', and green 'go', like traffic lights. Yellow might mean sunshine and happiness, blue might represent the sea. This prayer experiment uses colour to remind us of different reasons for praying.

Here are some ideas for prayer colours. You will probably be able to think of others.

- **RED** for sorry — things you want to stop doing.
- **YELLOW** for thank you — things that make you happy.
- **PINK** for please — things you want in the world.
- **BLUE** for other people — who might be 'feeling blue'.
- **GREEN** for the world — nature and our planet.

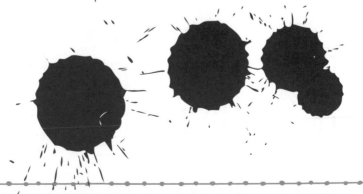

THE EXPERIMENT

Make a paper chain of prayers using different-coloured pieces of paper to represent different types of prayer. Use the colour ideas listed above or swap them around or make up your own categories.

YOU WILL NEED: Coloured paper and glue or sticky tape.

1 Cut out strips of different-coloured paper. A good size for the strips would be about 20 cm x 5 cm. You will probably need four or five of each colour. Choose the type of prayer each colour reminds you of.

2 Think of the type of prayer you'd like to pray and choose a paper strip in the correct colour to match that prayer. Write or draw your prayer on the paper. For example, if you want to pray for the world, you might draw a picture of an animal you want to thank God for.

3 Glue the ends of the strip together to make a circle.

4   When you pray another prayer, choose
    another strip in the correct colour and
    write or draw that prayer, then slip your
    new strip through the first circle and glue
    or tape the ends together to form a 'link'.

5   Keep praying more prayers and adding to
    your prayer paper chain!

MY NOTES

When I tried this...

Things I found most helpful were...

Things I might do differently next time were...

Marks out of 10:

WHAT OTHER EXPERIMENTERS THOUGHT

Tara (12) This was a great activity to do and one that I can grow with different prayers. I have done a similar activity with jelly beans, but I ate them. I can keep this and it looks good and my friends have asked about it. They want to know what the different colours are for and they liked that they could choose their own colours and they mean different things to different people. 9/10

Lucy (9) When I did this I felt different things as I was doing the different colours — I felt sort of caring and that I regretted the things I'd done wrong. It did help to show me and help me understand more how I was feeling, and I think the different colours helped with that. But a lot of the time my mind sort of went blank. 7/10

Marco (7) I did a red one for what I'm sorry for and a green one for the world — I wrote 'No pollution' on the green one. I liked the idea of the colours, but I got a bit bored writing the prayers, so I only did two. 2/10

Grace (8) I found it really fun. I looked at the colours and made a prayer that they reminded me of. Green made me think of grass so I prayed, 'Help us to keep the environment clean.' Other prayers I prayed were, 'I'm sorry I ask for stuff I don't need' and 'Thank you for giving me confidence in myself.' The thing I liked best was the rainbow colours. 9/10

'GOD IS GREAT' COLLAGE

'GOD IS GREAT' COLLAGE

God is amazing! For thousands of years, people have been praising God and writing poetry about how great God is. Some people enjoy using pictures and colour to show how brilliant they think God is. Fantastic colours and amazing pictures can help us to thank God for all the things he has made and given us. Just looking at something really beautiful and awe-inspiring can help us to contemplate God and just how amazing he is. This is something that is really hard to put into words, so sometimes it can be good to try thinking about God using colour and pictures rather than words.

This experiment involves making a collage to represent how you might describe God and creation. You might like to think about these questions to get you started.

★ What is God like?

★ How does God make you feel?

★ What words would you use to describe God?

★ What would you most like to say to God?

★ How has God helped you?

★ What has God made that you really want to say thank you for?

★ What colours and patterns remind you of God?

THE EXPERIMENT

Using colour and pictures can help us to think about God in a way that is beyond words. Create a 'God is great' collage to help you thank God for how amazing he is and for all the things he has made.

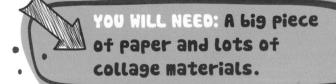

YOU WILL NEED: A big piece of paper and lots of collage materials.

1 Lay your big piece of paper on a flat surface. Use your collection of art materials – these could

include coloured and patterned
paper, glitter, stickers, buttons,
foil, sequins, tissue paper, wool,
felt-tip pens, pictures from
magazines or printed out from
the computer, together with glue
and scissors – to make a collage about how
great God is. Cover the whole piece of paper
if you can. Stick things on or draw straight
on to the paper.

2 Here are some ideas to help
you think of what you might
want to do.

✂ Draw pictures of what
you think God might look like

✂ Write and colour words to describe God.

✂ Cut out pictures of things
from creation that you love,
such as trees, animals or birds.

✂ Use colours and patterns that make
you think of God.

3 When you have finished, find somewhere to
hang your collage that will mean you can
see it every day.

4 As an alternative way of doing this,
you could try making a digital
slideshow or collage on the
computer, then print it out or
show it to friends and family.

MY NOTES

When I tried this...

_____

_____

_____

Things I found most helpful were...

_____

_____

_____

Things I might do differently next time were...

_____

_____

_____

Marks out of 10:

WHAT OTHER EXPERIMENTERS THOUGHT

Noah (12) I did this as a slideshow, because doing it electronically meant it was easier to find the pictures. Doing it as an actual collage might feel a bit babyish, though I suppose it might be fun to pretend to be a little kid again, cutting and sticking! I really enjoyed doing it on the computer, and it meant there was no limit to the pictures I could choose. To think about what pictures I wanted to use I had to really think, 'What reminds me of God?', so that made it of higher spiritual value. I thought about when I have felt a sense of the world being so much bigger than me and what makes me happy. 7/10

Emma (11) I made a digital collage by googling different landscapes around the world. Each landscape is unique and people have different needs as to where they live. I also looked at pictures of nature and I thought about nature and how no tree is the same and also rainbows are never the same. I associate this with good because everything is unique. Next time I could explore other ways that God is amazing. 9/10

Tara (12) I don't think I've visualized God before and I find it impossible to humanize God. It was fun to make, just using colours and cutting out pictures. The difficulty is where to put it and I don't find it helps me to pray. I think it would be a great activity for a group to do together and display at church or school. 6/10

Poppy (11) and Joss (9) did this together.

Poppy: It was really, really fun to do. We thought about how we could make words and patterns to represent God. We looked at what would contrast and what would go well. We put a lighthouse in the middle made of two plastic cups, electrical tape and a battery tea light. We liked the idea of God being like a lighthouse. I like the glitter glue we put on top of all the patterns to show God is special. I like how the patterns are all completely different, a bit like how you can see God in different ways. 10/10

Joss: The lighthouse is like a beacon of light calling out to everyone else. Our lighthouse is supposed to be God. He is stopping everyone from hitting sin like a lighthouse is stopping people hitting the rocks in the sea. We put gold glitter on to show God and his light providing for everyone. The red glitter is supposed to be the sin trying to get in, but it couldn't because the light is too powerful. It also looks like drops of blood, which reminds me of Jesus. 10/10

LEGO BIBLE MODELLING

LEGO BIBLE MODELLING

In the Bible itself, spending time reading the Bible is described as being like a tree, with our roots going deep into the soil, drinking up the life-giving water. If we spend time 'drinking in' the Bible we become deeply rooted, fed, stable and fruitful.

Spending time with the Bible doesn't have to mean always agreeing with it. Reading the Bible prayerfully is not about deciding whether it is true or not, or doing what it says. It is simply about spending time with the stories there, and seeing what they say to us about God, about the world and about ourselves.

One way to pray with a Bible story is to read it and then imagine yourself there.

○ What does it feel like? Hot? Cold? Windy? Is there sand between your toes or are you on rough grass?

○ What does it smell like? Animals? Flowers? Cooking?

○ What does it sound like? A busy crowd? Shouting? Silence? Birdsong? Water lapping at the seashore?

○ What does it look like? What can you see?

Imagine yourself in the scene. Who is there? What about you yourself — what part are you playing? Are you a bystander or one of the characters in the scene? Now imagine Jesus turning to you. What does he say?

This experiment is a bit like that, but less 'sit still and think' and more 'get out the Lego and build'.

THE EXPERIMENT

You are going to recreate, in Lego, a scene that tells a story from the Bible. The challenge isn't just to work out what the scene would have looked like. You also need to think about what the characters in the story are thinking or feeling, so try to choose Lego figures with appropriate facial expressions and pose them in a way that expresses what they might be feeling.

YOU WILL NEED: A Bible and some Lego.

1 The first thing you need to do is choose a Bible story. Some are suggested below, but choose something else if you prefer — maybe one of the readings you have heard in church or assembly recently or you could ask a parent, youth leader or minister to suggest one for you.

2 Decide whether you want to model the whole story or just one scene from it. If you are modelling the whole thing, you could take a series of photographs of the different scenes as you go and create a sort of

photo cartoon strip. You could even take
lots of photos and try putting them into
some stop-motion animation software,
to make a short animation of the story.
If you do this, why not offer it to school
or your local church for them to show
in assembly or a service, instead of just
reading the story?

3 When you have finished, you could show
your model, or photographs, to friends
and family. If you have a group of friends
to do this with, it can be fun to each try
modelling the same story, see how different
your models are and discuss why.

Here are some stories that other people have enjoyed modelling and where you can find them in the Bible.

JESUS CALMS THE STORM (MATTHEW 8.23–27, NRSV)

When Jesus got into the boat, his disciples followed him. A gale arose on the lake, so great that the boat was being swamped by the waves; but he was asleep. And they went and woke him up, saying, 'Lord, save us! We are perishing!' And he said to them, 'Why are you afraid, you of little faith?' Then he got up and rebuked the winds and the sea; and there was a dead calm. They were amazed, saying, 'What sort of man is this, that even the winds and the sea obey him?'

JESUS HAS OINTMENT (PERFUME) POURED OVER HIM (MARK 14.3–9, NRSV)

While Jesus was at Bethany in the house of Simon the leper, as he sat at the table, a woman came with an alabaster jar of very costly ointment of nard, and she broke open the jar and poured the ointment on his head. But some were there who said to one another in anger, 'Why was the ointment wasted in this way? For this ointment could have been sold for more than three hundred denarii, and the money given to the poor.' And they scolded her. But Jesus said, 'Let her alone; why do you trouble her? She has performed a good service for me. For you always have the poor with you, and you can show kindness to them whenever you wish; but you will not always have me. She has done what she could; she has anointed my body beforehand for its burial. Truly I tell you, wherever the good news is proclaimed in the whole world, what she has done will be told in remembrance of her.'

THE PARABLE OF THE GOOD SAMARITAN (LUKE 10.30–35, NIV)

A man was going down from Jerusalem to Jericho, when he was attacked by robbers. They stripped him of his clothes, beat him and went away, leaving him half-dead. A priest happened to be going down the same road, and when he saw the man, he passed by on the other side. So too, a Levite, when he came to the place and saw him, passed by on the other side. But a Samaritan, as he travelled, came where the man was; and when he saw him, he took pity on him. He went to him and bandaged his wounds, pouring on oil and wine. Then he put the man on his own donkey, brought him to an inn and took care of him. The next day he took out two denarii and gave them to the innkeeper.

'Look after him,' he said, 'and when I return,
I will reimburse you for any extra expense you
may have.'

JESUS APPEARS TO HIS DISCIPLES AFTER THE RESURRECTION (JOHN 20.19–22, NRSV)

When it was evening on that day, the first day of
the week, and the doors of the house where the
disciples had met were locked for fear of the Jews,
Jesus came and stood among them and said, 'Peace
be with you.' After he said this, he showed them
his hands and his side. Then the disciples rejoiced
when they saw the Lord. Jesus said to them again,
'Peace be with you. As the Father has sent me, so
I send you.' When he had said this, he breathed on
them and said to them, 'Receive the Holy Spirit.'

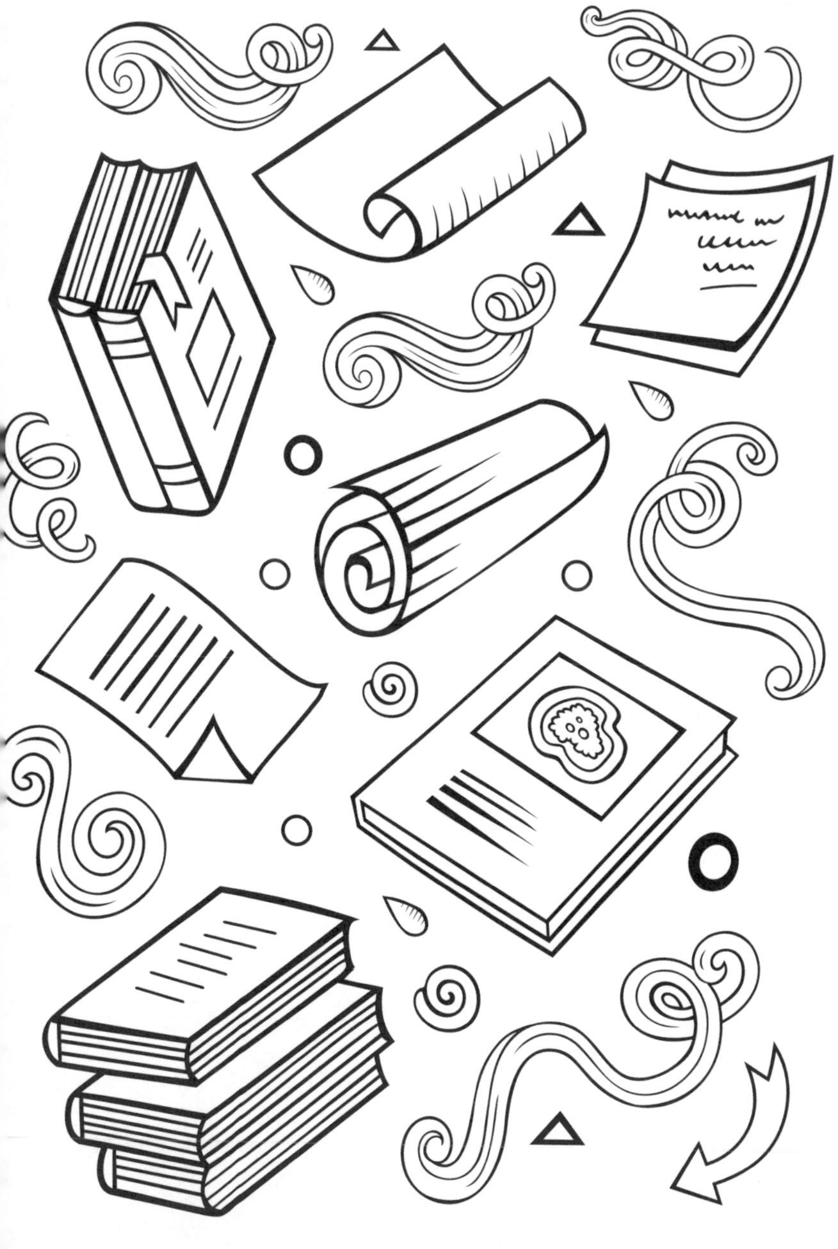

MY NOTES

When I tried this...

Things I found most helpful were...

Things I might do differently next time were...

Marks out of 10:

WHAT OTHER EXPERIMENTERS THOUGHT

Alex (11) Lego is really fun anyway, but putting it to a Christian purpose was really great. I made the Easter scene. It was quite easy to make, but then I liked how you could move the pieces and re-enact it. 6/10

Solomon (7) It was really fun finding the pieces and building it. I was really glad when we finished because it took quite a long time but it was worth it. The best bit was looking at it at the end. The time it took us was about two hours. Afterwards we could just relax. 9/10

Poppy (11) I thought it was fun looking at all the parts of Lego and seeing what we could do for the scene. 9/10

Joss (9) I really enjoyed mixing things to make a scene. We had Joseph kneeling down before the pharaoh with two guards either side of him and a mini jail in the background and the butler and baker either side of it. I really enjoyed finding all the right bricks because it's more fun when you have to find the bricks yourself. It gave me a different view of the story. 8/10

Toby (9) I really liked doing this. I did the story of the Good Samaritan, and I made a model of the Samaritan taking the man who was attacked to the inn. I had him on a stretcher as I couldn't find or make a donkey, and then a bed in the inn. I built a desk for the innkeeper and had the Samaritan giving him money to look after the stranger. It really made me think about the story. 9/10

PRAYER TREE

PRAYER TREE

When we think
about what prayer is,
asking God for things is probably
the first thing most people think of. Of course
it is OK to ask God for anything that is on your
mind! The Bible is full of examples of people
asking for what they most want, from good
things like food, water and justice to bad things
like revenge. On a particular day you might want
to ask God to make situations that you've heard
about around the world better, to help you with a
friend you've had an argument with and help you

do well in a test or exam. You might want to pray for a friend or relation who is ill, asking God to make that person better. You might be feeling anxious or scared about something and ask God both to change the situation and to give you a feeling of calm about it.

Basically, all you need to do is be honest. Tell God what you are really feeling, what you are unhappy about, what you want more than anything in the world. You can trust God to know if something you are asking for would be bad for you or for other people and do what is the most loving thing.

We know from the Bible that God can intervene in the world to change things, but also that it is quite unusual for miracles to happen. So it is worth praying for things that seem impossible, but be prepared for your prayers to be answered in ways other than what you expected or were hoping for. For example, not everyone we pray for who is ill will get better — everyone dies at some time — but we can still trust that God will hear our prayers and help them to die at peace and be with God in heaven after they die and comfort those who are sad.

THE EXPERIMENT

Make a prayer tree to help you remember people and situations you would like to ask God's help for, and use it to guide your prayers.

YOU WILL NEED: A vase or jam jar, twigs and gift tags.

1 Gather some twigs and stand them in a vase or jam jar. Or you could use a fairly substantial potted plant for this or even a jewellery tree.

2 Now prepare some little notes to hang on the twigs. The easiest thing is to use gift tags with a hanging loop of thread already attached. Or use pieces of paper, either plain or cut out to look like leaves. Use a hole punch or a sharp pencil to make a hole in each one and tie on a loop of thread, wool or gift ribbon.

3 Write a person or situation that you want to

ask God's help for on each of the tags and
hang them on the tree, consciously giving
that person or situation to God and handing
over your worry to God as you do so.

4 Place your tree somewhere in your room.
You might want to pray through each of the
tags every day or once a week. You can add
new ones whenever you like and when one
of them no longer needs to be prayed for,
you can remove the tag from the tree. You
could keep any prayers that you feel have
been answered in a box. If you keep adding
to the tree regularly, this box could
then become a lovely record
of answered prayers.

MY NOTES

When I tried this...

Things I found most helpful were...

Things I might do differently next time were...

Marks out of 10:

WHAT OTHER EXPERIMENTERS THOUGHT

Alex (11) We used a vase and loads of white sticks. We prayed for people to get better and for people all over the world. The cat tipped it over. She would probably give it a 10! 9/10

Daniel (11) I used a small tree growing in a pot and some small sticky notes. I wrote the prayers on the notes and stuck them on the leaves of the tree. I had it representing that when the notes fell off the tree, the prayer would be answered. I couldn't think of what to pray for, so I prayed for stopping a war that's in the news a lot at the moment, and providing food for the poor who need it. I felt my prayers were being listened to by God. 9/10

Noah (12) I thought this was really good because of the interactivity of going and getting the sticks and actually making the tree. That made it feel more personal. The concept of a tree is giving people life, because trees give out oxygen, so making a prayer tree to pray for people linked together really well. I made little tags, hole-punched them and hung them on the tree with bits of wool. On each one I drew a picture or cut out a shape to symbolize what I was praying for, then wrote on the other side. Putting the prayers on to the tree it felt a bit like I was actually giving the people life and hope. It felt as if God was somehow in the tree, looking at the people I was putting on it and praying with me for them. 9/10

BEDHEAD
PRAYER
POSTER

BEDHEAD PRAYER POSTER

Do you have posters and pictures on your bedroom walls or door? They probably say something about who you are and what your interests are.

In many religious traditions, written prayers or short blessings are put on doorways or on the

walls of rooms. These may ask God to bless the house or room, then every time you go into that room, you are reminded to pray. You don't even have to consciously say the prayer each time; you just see it and notice it as you are passing.

There is a long tradition in Christianity of praying when you get up in the morning and before you go to bed at night. Doing this means you 'frame' your whole day with prayer. It can help you remember God through the day. You can ask for God's help in the morning with anything that worries you about the day to come, and at the end of the day you can say thank you for what has gone well, say sorry for anything you have done wrong and pray for God's help for people or things that you have seen through the day.

The poster you make in this experiment can be a way of helping you to pray when you get up in the morning and also in the evening when you might be too tired to think of something to say.

THE EXPERIMENT

Try making a prayer poster to go above your bed. Just seeing it will remind you about God, and reading the prayer on it is a really easy way to pray. You could do two — one for the morning and one for the evening — or just one.

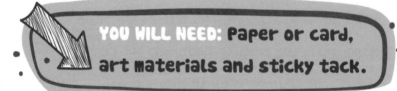

YOU WILL NEED: Paper or card, art materials and sticky tack.

1 First, think about what you want your poster to say. You might ask God to bless you in your room, help you as you sleep, be

with you through the day or a combination
of lots of different things!

2 When you've decided, write the words out. Make
   sure the writing is quite big, so you can read
   it when you walk into the room or when you
   are lying in bed. Then decorate the poster with
   coloured pens, pictures, stickers and glitter.
   Make it something you will enjoy seeing.

3 Stick the poster to the wall in your
   bedroom, above your bed, where you will see
   it every time you get into and out of bed.

4 Leave it there for at least a week. For the
   first day or two, deliberately say the prayer
   every time you see it.

MY NOTES

When I tried this...

Things I found most helpful were...

Things I might do differently next time were...

Marks out of 10:

WHAT OTHER EXPERIMENTERS THOUGHT

Zoë (8) I always thought it was quite scary going to sleep at night, so I decided to make a little prayer to put up above my bed. Every night when I go to bed, sometimes after my bedtime story, I say that prayer. Some of it is about nightmares going away and it helps me to go to sleep without worrying about nightmares. I feel just calm when I say the prayer — I'm in my own little zone in the world and it's like there's no one around me. Even if I don't say the prayer, I think having it on the wall means I know it's there so I can say it if I feel scared. 10/10

Tara (12) This reminded me to pray each night. Having pictures and colour on it made it stand out and made me happy to pray. Better than just boring words or having nothing to say. 8/10

Hannah (10) I put this on the curtain covering my door. After a while, it kept getting in the way so I removed it, but I had got used to saying it in my head and I say the prayer going out of the door automatically now. 7/10

Grace (8) I made two posters. One was asking God to help me be confident. One was saying thank you for the lady who made up fidget spinners. I think it's important to pray because without God we wouldn't have the world and we pray so we can say thank you to God. There was nothing I didn't like about this one. I'm going to put both above my bed. I will choose which one to say each night. If I'm in a really good mood I might say both of them. 10/10

BUBBLE WRAP WORRY PRAYERS

BUBBLE WRAP WORRY PRAYERS

Sometimes life can be a bit scary and we have to do things or think about things that make us worried. Jesus doesn't want us to be afraid and it can often be very helpful to pray about our worries and ask him to help us.

In the Bible, Jesus tells his disciples many times not to be afraid. In one story, Jesus is asleep in a boat on a stormy sea and his friends are terrified, so they wake him up. Jesus stops the storm and the disciples realize that he has the power to keep them safe.

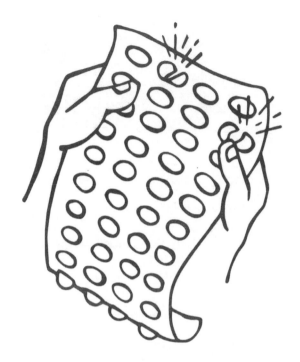

I love bubble wrap! Not just because it is great to pop but also because if I wrap something in it, the item will be protected.

In this experiment we use bubble wrap as a way of praying about our worries and giving them to God.

THE EXPERIMENT

When you are feeling afraid or worried about something, try using bubble wrap while you are praying to God about it. The idea is to give your fears and worries to God and ask him to keep you safe.

YOU WILL NEED: A sheet of bubble wrap.

1 Think about something that you are afraid of or is worrying you. Holding the bubble wrap, tell God what it is and ask him to help you not to feel afraid or worried. If it makes sense, ask God to keep you safe.

2 Pop a bubble to show that you have given your worry to God.

3 If you have more than one worry or fear, do the same for each one.

MY NOTES

When I tried this...

Things I found most helpful were...

Things I might do differently next time were...

Marks out of 10:

WHAT OTHER EXPERIMENTERS THOUGHT

Alex (11) I found it really cool because bubble wrap is my favourite thing. It works really well. I liked it because it's really interesting. I liked how you popped it and you felt the pops were going to God and it was a really calm time. 6/10

Poppy (11) It was really comforting to pop the bubbles while praying. I really liked it. It was really calming just to pop the bubbles because it was nice to feel the air going out from under your fingers. It was good to hold the bubble wrap and move while you were praying. 9/10

Joss (9) I felt really close to God. When I popped one of the bubbles it sort of felt soothing in a way. It helped me with my worries. 7/10

Tobias (12) It really does work. You think of something, then you ask God to help you and when you pop the bubble it genuinely does feel like you've just popped that worry away. It felt really calming. 10/10

Zoë (8) When you pop it, the worries don't totally go away, but they go to the back of your mind. I felt really calm, like a candle has been lit and you're in church. It felt good to be praying quietly but it was also really fun, popping the bubbles. 10/10

CONTEMPLATION BOTTLES

CONTEMPLATION BOTTLES

Prayer is not always just about the words we say.
For thousands of years, people have
found it useful to pray in silence and
think about God on their own.
We know that Jesus often
went away by himself to pray
and in the Bible it tells us
that sometimes it is good to
be 'still' and focus on God.
Sometimes we need a
bit of help to settle into

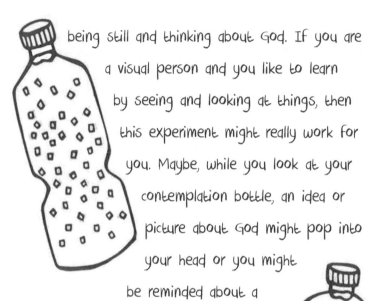

being still and thinking about God. If you are a visual person and you like to learn by seeing and looking at things, then this experiment might really work for you. Maybe, while you look at your contemplation bottle, an idea or picture about God might pop into your head or you might be reminded about a Bible story you know. You might be surprised at what comes to you in the silence!

THE EXPERIMENT

Make a contemplation bottle with water and glitter to help you be still and think about God. Sitting in a quiet and comfortable space, watch the glitter swirl in the bottle and, after a few times, perhaps note down what comes into your mind.

YOU WILL NEED: A clear plastic bottle and some glitter.

1 Pour two tablespoons of glitter into your bottle (this works really well if you use two different colours) and then fill the bottle with water. You could add a few teaspoons

of glycerine or honey to the water to make
it thicker so that the glitter takes longer
to settle than it does in just water. Screw
the bottle lid on tightly.

2 Find a comfortable place to sit where
   you will not be disturbed — maybe
   somewhere with lots of cushions.

3 Shake the bottle and watch the glitter
   swirl around then finally settle. Use the
   time you are watching this happen to think
   about God. Does anything come into your
   mind? Does God say anything to you?

4 If you like, when you are ready, write a note
   about anything that comes to you.

MY NOTES

When I tried this...

Things I found most helpful were...

Things I might do differently next time were...

Marks out of 10:

WHAT OTHER EXPERIMENTERS THOUGHT

Tobias (12) When you shake it up it goes quite fast, and I found it hard to concentrate as everything was moving so fast. But then as it slows down towards the end, it's more contemplative. Thoughts that came to my mind were: gentle, kind, peaceful; recognizing that we take time to sort things out when they are scrambled; and God lets us choose our own path. 8/10

Zoë (8) When I was looking at the bottle it felt calm, as if it was God's Spirit in the bottle instead of glitter. Mostly what I was thinking inside my head was, 'God is awesome, God is cool'! When I was making the bottle I wondered how this was going to remind me of God, and I thought it would probably be boring. But when I watched it, all my thoughts seemed to zoom away and I was just there in the room alone, but there was someone there. The Holy Spirit was zooming around the room and I'd never be alone because God was there. 7/10

Solomon (7) We put red and gold glitter into the bottle. With the red glitter I thought about the bad things in the world to pray about and with the gold glitter the good things in the world to pray about. When you shake the bottle to make a tornado, I prayed about places where destruction was taking place, like Syria, Israel. I have it on my bedside table now. 10/10

Alex (11) I put a piece of foil in there and some small glitter. The foil was God and the glitter was us. It made me think about how God is always there and how we sometimes try to get away from God but we can't! 8/10

MINECRAFT
CHURCH

MINECRAFT CHURCH

We can pray to God anywhere, but sometimes people find going to a special place like a church helps. A place set aside for praying in can be somewhere you feel at peace or closer to God or just anywhere that is different from everyday life.

Like a church, virtual world computer games such as Minecraft are somewhere outside our day-to-day lives. They are places where we can get away from the usual for a bit, places where we might meet friends, imagine ourselves differently and try new things.

Virtual worlds can be very creative places, as

we are free to express ourselves and build almost anything we can imagine. So they are good places to experiment and try things out.

This experiment involves creating a prayer space in Minecraft — or any other virtual world-building game that you enjoy and are familiar with — then imagining yourself praying in it.

In these games, one thing to watch out for is the combat element in some versions. It doesn't create a very prayerful atmosphere if you are having to fight off zombies or giant spiders. So we suggest that you do this experiment in Creative rather than Survival mode or on Peaceful settings to avoid monsters disturbing you!

As you plan what to build, think about what your ideal place for prayer could be like.

- ☐ Where will it be?
- ☐ What views will it have?
- ☐ What will it be made of?
- ☐ What will it look like?
- ☐ How big or small should it be?
- ☐ What could it have inside it?
- ☐ What will you do there?

THE EXPERIMENT

Using Minecraft or another similar game, create your own personal prayer space. Once you have made it, try going into it in your character in the game and praying there. Will you pray for the same things you pray for in this world or different things?

YOU WILL NEED: Minecraft or other virtual world-building game.

1 Plan what you would like your ideal personal prayer space to look like. Ask yourself the questions listed in the introduction to this experiment and think about every detail.

2 Now go online and have a go at making your dream prayer space. It might be a virtual church, chapel or cathedral, or it could look completely different. Some people who have tried this have made very traditional-looking churches, while others have made anything from floating platforms in glass boxes to tiny houses.

3 Once you've built it, try going into it, as your virtual character,

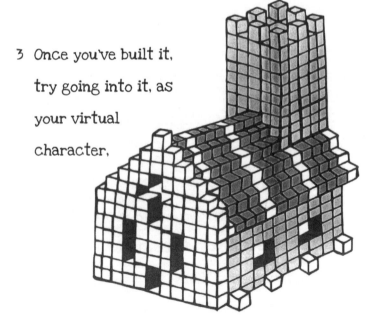

and spend some time praying there.
Is it any different from being in a chapel,
church or prayer space in the real world?
If so, how? Did you act differently in the
space that you made yourself than you
would in a real church? What did you pray
for? We have found that people often take
on the role of a vicar or take charge of
leading the prayers in their Minecraft
churches, because it feels like their
space! Do you imagine yourself alone in
the space or will you bring other people or
characters in?

MY NOTES

When I tried this...

_____

_____

_____

Things I found most helpful were...

_____

_____

_____

Things I might do differently next time were...

_____

_____

_____

Marks out of 10:

WHAT OTHER EXPERIMENTERS THOUGHT

Joss (9) I put so much work into it but I still loved it. I felt that when I was doing something associated with God my work was better. I had the main room with the font, the pews and also I had placed someone behind the altar. They were picking up the cup and the tiny bit of bread. 8/10

Poppy (11) I really enjoyed exploring the things that I was able to do on Minecraft to make my church. I wanted to make it really exciting. I did rainbow pews. I was able to put notices up. I wrote 'Welcome to the church.' 9/10

Phoebe (11) with her brother Ben (8) It was quite fun and creative making it, then you can calm down from anything that's worrying you when you go into it. Because your mind is in a creative mood when you are in Minecraft it is easier to think and pray than at other times. We made a big church, a big rectangle with a roof and two floors. It had a font, organ, altar, pews, a pulpit, hymn boards and a cross. We got all the villagers into the pews and choir stalls, and I went into the pulpit and prayed. I prayed for the things that the people in Minecraft would need; for them, their enemies, like the Creepers, and their crops and so on. Doing it in Minecraft meant that I thought of the things that were relevant there, but then I prayed for those sorts of things in real life too — people with enemies and not enough food to eat and animals. My brother was the organist, so his character was sitting at the organ and he wiggled his fingers in real life to be 'playing' the organ while we all sang lots of hymns. 8/10

ROUGH TIMES
SANDPAPER
PRAYERS

ROUGH TIMES
SANDPAPER PRAYERS

In the Bible, the desert is often seen as a place of testing and trouble. It is a place where people have rough times, but where God is always with them. The Israelites wandered in the desert for 40 years before they came to the promised land, but God fed them and kept them safe.

Even Jesus had a hard time in the desert wilderness. As we remember in Lent, Jesus once spent 40 days praying in the desert and not eating anything. Although it was a very hard time, when he felt that he was being tested to his limits, he found that God gave him the strength to manage.

In this experiment, the rough feel of sandpaper is a good reminder of both the difficult times that we experience in life and the sandy, dry desert of those Bible stories. The colour and soft texture of wool helps us to think of the life and protection that God brought to his people, and will also give to us when we are having a hard time.

THE EXPERIMENT

This experiment can help remind us that God offers comfort and protection in the difficult times of life. The sandpaper helps us think of deserts and rough times, then the soft wool represents God's blessing in answer to our prayers.

YOU WILL NEED: Sandpaper and different-coloured lengths of wool (each about 5 cm long).

1 Feel the roughness of a piece of sandpaper. What does it remind you of? Which stories from the Bible do you know where people

were having a difficult time but God brought
a change and a new start for them?

2 Think about times from your life when
things have been rough. Have you ever
asked God to help you?

3 Still feeling the sandpaper, think about
people you know who are going through
rough, difficult times at the moment. Ask
God to help and bless them.

4 As you pray for yourself and other people,
arrange the soft, different-coloured
lengths of wool on the sandpaper as a sign
of the new life and change you are asking
God to bring.

MY NOTES

When I tried this...

Things I found most helpful were...

Things I might do differently next time were...

Marks out of 10:

WHAT OTHER EXPERIMENTERS THOUGHT

Joss (9) I was reminded of the three children who live in Uganda and we sponsor. When I felt the rough sandpaper it made me think of all the people who have been having a rough time and I thought of them and hopefully that their lives would get better and they would get more education. 7/10

Tobias (12) I think this works really well because it helps you to realize how lucky you are and really appreciate what God has done for you. It also helped me appreciate the rough times others are going through. 6/10

Alex (11) I found it really good because you could make a scene from the Bible and when you took the wool off, the sandpaper wouldn't feel as rough. 7/10

Poppy (11) I enjoyed having a quiet time praying for people while feeling the sandpaper. When I was feeling the paper I thought about how hard people's lives are and what we take for granted and how some people, without you knowing, are having a much harder time than you. 8/10

Zoë (8) It helped me remember that, at first, the world was plain, but God made it bright and beautiful. The yellow wool that I put on represents the light that shines in our world, the purple represents beauty, the pink represents animals, the blue represents the sea and the green represents the land — all together making one beautiful planet. Then I made a rainbow.
7/10

PRAYING
WITH YOUR
BODY

PRAYING WITH YOUR BODY

How much do you think about what you do with your body when you pray? Scientists are continually finding more connections between our bodies and our minds. We are not just a mind in a body, like a computer in a case. Our bodies are part of us and what we do with our bodies can shape our thinking.

Try this: smile. You actually feel happier when you make the muscle movements that are a smile, even if you are just acting.

How many different physical ways of praying can you think of?

Originally, in the days of the early Church in Roman times, people seem to have stood to pray, with their arms outstretched. If you go to church, you may see that the position of the priest during the Communion prayer is a reminder of this.

Kneeling became fashionable in the Middle Ages. It was a position that people were familiar with, because you had to kneel before a lord or the king or queen, so people found it natural to relate to God as they would to their earthy superior.

In some times and places, people lie on the floor to pray. This is called prostration. People usually do it only at particularly serious times of prayer. In the past, monks or nuns might have prayed all night lying on the floor before taking vows to join the monastery, and a knight might have done the same before a battle.

Nowadays, the most common posture for prayer is sitting down. Differences are mostly about what you do with your hands. Clasped together? Flat together? Open on your knees, as if you were waiting to receive something from God? In the air, as if you were getting carried away at a rock concert or celebrating a goal?

THE EXPERIMENT

In this experiment, try out several different postures for prayer and see how they make you feel about the relationship between you and God.

1 Go somewhere you know you won't be disturbed, like your bedroom, so you won't feel embarrassed at being found in different positions! Then try standing with your arms out (like a priest at the altar). Imagine you are standing before God. How does it feel to be in front of God like this?

2 Next, kneel down (on just one or both knees). This might feel like kneeling before the monarch to be knighted or pleading with someone for a favour or mercy. Imagine you are kneeling in front of God. How does it feel?

3 Now lie down, flat on your front, legs together, arms outstretched — a bit like a lying-down crucifix. Are you lying in front of God? How does that feel? Are you imagining what it was like for Christ on the cross?

4 Now sit on a chair or on the side of your bed. Imagine Jesus sitting next to you.

How does it feel to be talking to God in this position? If you like, try out some different hand positions too.

5 If your body comes up with other ideas for positions, then try those out as well. Think about how each position makes you feel and how it makes you feel in relation to God if you imagine God there in the room with you.

MY NOTES

When I tried this...

Things I found most helpful were...

Things I might do differently next time were...

Marks out of 10:

WHAT OTHER EXPERIMENTERS THOUGHT

Joss (9) Standing made me feel open, kneeling made me feel responsible, lying down made me feel harmed. Sitting made me feel close to Jesus. What I liked most was sitting down in a chair because I felt close to Jesus. Because of doing this, we now have a special chair we can sit on to pray. 8.5/10

Noah (12) I tried standing first. It was probably the one where if God was actually in front of me, I'd be most shocked. Standing felt more vulnerable — vulnerable to God's power. If you were standing before God what would he say to you? When I was kneeling it felt like an interview with God: I felt small, with no protection. I imagined a picture in my head, in heaven — kneel here in front of God's big desk, and he starts interviewing you and telling you all the wrong things you've done in your life and the few good things you've done. And all the time I'm hoping God will let me into heaven — which he probably would, because he forgives, but it was still pretty horrible. Sitting down was the easiest, because it was much more relaxing. I didn't have such a strong picture in my head as I felt much more relaxed. God was there, but I was just getting on with praying in front of God. Lying down was really strange but definitely my favourite because of what happened. For the first minute or so I was just settling down and trying to close down my senses and stuff and imagine God, so I was saying the Lord's Prayer. Then it was as if there was a bright light over my bed and a voice saying the Lord's Prayer with me. That only lasted quite briefly and I lay there for a bit longer, hoping it would come back, but nothing more happened. That was a lovely experience and I'd really like it to happen again. 9.5/10

PRAYER
TYPES
CHATTERBOX

PRAYER TYPES CHATTERBOX

Have you ever made chatterboxes at school? I would be very surprised if you've never seen or played with one before. They are very easy to make with a square of paper, once you get the hang of the folding, and are a great way to pray if you like to do things with your hands. You also have the chance to pray lots of different types of prayer. To get the most out of this activity, you need to do the experiment with someone else.

THE EXPERIMENT

You can make a chatterbox using the template here or make up your own version, then use it to make up some fun prayers with family or friends.

YOU WILL NEED: A printable chatterbox template

(<https://docs.google.com/file/d/0B0RweH-3Ryl0b0hlRUxiU0RlYjQ/edit>).

1 First, cut off the excess paper so that you are left with the chatterbox square.

2 Fold the square into a chatterbox (there are instructions on the internet if you haven't done this before).

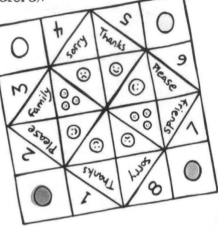

3 Now it is ready to use, find a friend to pray with you. Ask your friend to choose one of the four colours. Spell the name of the colour and push the chatterbox together and apart each time you say a letter.

4 Now ask your friend to choose a number from the ones shown on the inside of

the chatterbox.
Count up to that
number, pushing the
chatterbox together

and apart each time you say a number.

5 Now ask your friend to choose another
number, then lift up the flap. Pray the type
of prayer that is underneath.

6 If you are feeling adventurous, you might

like to make your
own version with
a new piece of
paper!

MY NOTES

When I tried this...

Things I found most helpful were...

Things I might do differently next time were...

Marks out of 10:

WHAT OTHER EXPERIMENTERS THOUGHT

Zoë (8) These are very useful because when you can't think what to pray about, you can just get it out and do it with friends or on your own. I had lots of fun making it because it is very cute. The different kinds of prayer are 'please', 'family', 'friends', 'sorry' and 'thanks'. When I got one I just said the first thing that popped into my head each time. 6/10

Tobias (12) The making of it didn't take long, but it could be annoying if you didn't get it right first time. I used it with my mum and on my own, and I found it worked much better doing it with someone else. It felt more like an atmosphere suitable for praying doing it with someone else. We took turns and that gave you time to think while the other person was doing it. It was helpful to be given a guideline for the type of prayer to pray, because quite often I find it hard to just sit down and pray. I don't know what to say, and also I find you tend to say way too many pleases. I will use this again, maybe once a week, with my mum or my sister. 9/10

Poppy (11) I liked the idea of praying using the chatterbox and it was fun seeing what people got. I liked it as a way of praying because it was exciting and fun as well because it was a bit like a game and you didn't know what type of prayer you would get. I played it with everyone in my family. They chose whether to pray out loud or in their head. 7/10

Alex (11) They were good when they were made, but were quite hard to make — very fiddly. I did it with my mum. I liked all the different decisions you have to make. I liked praying for people and the world best. 6/10

PRAYER DEN

PRAYER DEN

Praying in a big space has the advantage of making you feel part of something bigger than yourself. High ceilings and big spaces are designed to lift your eyes and mind to God's majesty, and make you feel very small in comparison. Praying in a public building makes the important point that we are not just individual Christians, but part of the worldwide Church.

However, a small space of your own can feel safe and more intimate than a large building. It can be somewhere to feel private with God. Somewhere you can be yourself without having to think about what other people might be thinking of you. A place where it feels like God comes to meet you rather than you having to go out to meet God.

You could make a prayer corner in your room. As you try the various experiments in this book, why not keep some of the things you make and put them together on a shelf or windowsill? Then you will build up your own personal collection of prayer objects and reminders and so create a prayer corner of your own.

The prayer den experiment takes that idea a step further, creating a small, enclosed space to pray in — just big enough for one or maybe two people.

THE EXPERIMENT

Your own private prayer den can be as simple or as elaborate as you like. You'll need to think about where to put your prayer den, what to make it out of and what to put in it.

1 First, where will you build your den? In the corner of your bedroom? Maybe in a family room, shed or garage? How about outside, if it is summer? Your den could be something that just stays up for an afternoon or else a semi-permanent den — whatever suits the space you have available.

2 The easiest way to create a den is to pitch
  a tent – perhaps a pop-up play tent, if you
  have one. Here are some other ideas: a
  bottom bunk bed, with sheets or blankets
  clipped to the bunk above; a clothes airer;
  pieces of furniture arranged to make an
  enclosed space (such as chests of drawers,
  chairs); a very large cardboard box; or a
  table.

3 Cover your chosen framework to make
   a completely enclosed space, perhaps
   using sheets, blankets or duvets. Make
   it comfortable to sit in for a reasonable
   length of time by covering the floor with
   pillows, cushions and beanbags, for example.

4 Now decide how to decorate your den inside!
   People who have tried this have particularly
   liked having fairy lights or a lava lamp.
   You could take a torch in with you. Just be
   careful to use only a low wattage lamp that
   doesn't get hot, to avoid any risk of fire.
   You might want to add other things –
   maybe items from your prayer corner,
   bunting or a rug. Make a space that feels

snug and secure, somewhere you will enjoy sitting in that feels very personal to you.

5 Once you have built the den, you can start using it to pray in. Just go in, sit down and imagine that God is in there with you. Sit quietly, imagining you are in the presence of God, or talk with God or say prayers that you know, such as the Lord's Prayer. You might like to have paper and pens with you to draw or write your prayers. Another idea is to try combining this with other experiments, doing one or two of the other prayer activities suggested here in the den.

MY NOTES

When I tried this...

Things I found most helpful were...

Things I might do differently next time were...

Marks out of 10:

WHAT OTHER EXPERIMENTERS THOUGHT

Alex (11) It's really great fun building a den and then praying in it. 9/10

Daniel (11) I liked the prayer den because it allowed me to have a small space that was very personal to me where I could pray. To make it I used a football goal with a duvet and some blankets draped over and some cushions on the floor. I brought in some objects that were special to me: a Bible, a globe and a small tree. Every night I would go in there and read a psalm aloud to myself and also pray about a few other things. It's a place to snuggle up and get warm, but most of all, it was a very nice idea. 10/10

Joss (9) I prayed for all the refugees and other people who are facing poverty. We used the glitter jar (see 'Contemplation bottles', page 97) in the tent. We put the red and gold glitter in. We shook it around and prayed with it. 8/10

Poppy (11) I really liked it and I quite liked the patterns on the duvet. I liked lying down and looking at the patterns. It was quite calming and it made me feel tired. 9/10

Solomon (7) We made it out of the ironing board, two duvets, two blankets, three wooden chairs and about ten cushions. I just looked around inside it. We prayed out loud. I prayed for refugees. 8/10

BONUS MATERIAL: GROUP ACTIVITIES

Here are even more prayer experiments for you to try. All these experiments use items that you are likely to find at home and most of them are good to do with other people. Think about who else in your family or church you could ask to join in with you!

BOXES PRAYERS

The 'BOX' game is very simple and is a great way to pass the time when you are waiting for something. This version of the game turns it into a prayer activity. The WINNER is the person who has filled the most boxes with prayers by the end of the game.

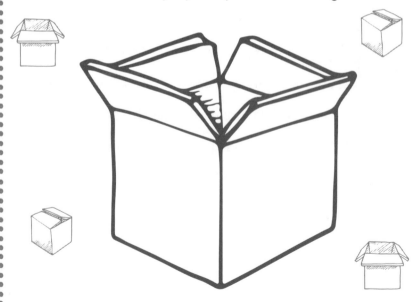

YOU WILL NEED: **Paper, pens or pencils (each player should have a different colour).**

1 Draw some dots in lines and columns on the paper (see below).

2 Each player takes it in turns to draw a line between two of the dots. The dots must be next door to each other and you can't draw diagonal lines.

3 Eventually, the lines you draw will start to make closed boxes. Whoever draws the line that closes the box can write or draw a prayer inside the box. You might want to pray by writing or drawing:

✎ someone's name — ask God to bless them and help them,

✎ something that you want to thank God for,

✎ something you would like to ask God for.

4 Take time to say the prayer out loud or in
  your head, then carry on with the game
  until all the boxes have been made and
  filled with prayers!

PIPE CLEANER PRAYERS

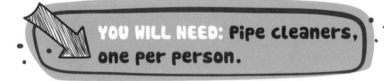his experiment is another way to pray for **OTHER PEOPLE**. You will probably really enjoy this way of praying if you like to do things with your hands.

YOU WILL NEED: Pipe cleaners, one per person.

1 Make your pipe cleaner into the initial letter of the name of someone you know. Ask God to bless that person.

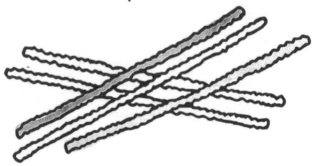

2 Make your pipe cleaner into the shape of
   something you would like to say thank you
   to God for.

3 Screw your pipe cleaner up and pray for
   people who are sick, confused or sad.

4 Link your pipe cleaner to someone else's
   and pray for people who are lonely.

5 Put your pipe cleaner around your wrist
   like a bracelet as a reminder that God is
   always with you.

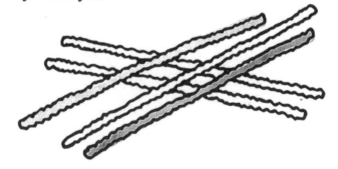

PLAYING CARD PRAYERS

t's quite likely that you will have a pack of **PLAYING CARDS** somewhere in your house. Here is a way of praying with the different types of cards you find in the pack.

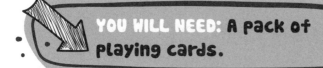

> YOU WILL NEED: A pack of
> playing cards.

1 Shuffle a pack of cards and
lay the pack face down on a
table or on the floor. Take it
in turns to take a card off
the top of the pile.

2 Each time you pick up a
card, look at the type of card it is and use
these ideas to help you pray:

♠ for a red number card, say a 'thank
you' prayer;

♣ for a black number card, say a 'sorry'
or 'please' prayer;

♠ for a king card, think of a word to describe God and how great he is,

♣ for a queen card, pray for someone who is female,

♠ for a Jack card, pray for someone who is male.

SALT PRAYERS

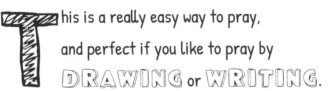his is a really easy way to pray, and perfect if you like to pray by **DRAWING** or **WRITING**.

If you don't have salt, you can use play sand instead.

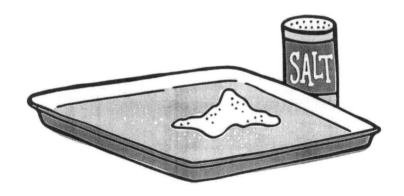

YOU WILL NEED: A tray with sides, table salt, lolly sticks.

1 Pour plenty of salt into a tray (such as a roasting tin) until the bottom is completely covered. Smooth out the salt to make the surface flat.

2 Use a lolly stick to write or draw your prayer in the salt. You might want to:

★ draw a person you know or write the initial letter of his or her name, then ask God to help and bless that person;

★ draw something you'd like to say thank you to God for;

★   draw or write something you'd like to
    ask God for;

★   draw or write something you're sorry for
    and ask God to forgive you.

3 As you say 'Amen' after each prayer, out
  loud or in your head, smooth the salt over
  again and repeat.

STRAW ROCKET PRAYERS

Sometimes when we pray it's really helpful to picture GIVING our prayer to God so we don't need to worry about it or hold on to it any more. This prayer experiment is a way to visually give your prayer to God and it's FUN!

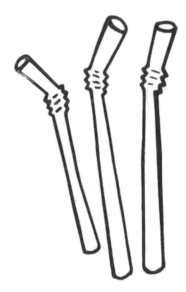

YOU WILL NEED: Bendy drinking straws, paper, sticky tape, pens.

1 Write or draw your prayer ('please', 'sorry' or 'thank you') on a small piece of paper (about 3 cm x 5 cm).

2 Roll the paper tightly round a straw (the long straight end rather than the bendy end) and secure it with sticky tape.

3 Push the rolled paper up the straw a little bit so that some of the paper is above the end of the straw.

4 Fold the top of the paper over and secure it
   with some more sticky tape. The paper will
   now have made a sealed pocket around the
   top end of the straw. Make sure this pocket
   is not too tight around the top of the straw
   or else the next part won't work!

5 Ask God to take your prayer, then say 'Amen'.

6 Blow through the bendy end of the straw.
   The paper at the other end should
   fly off like a rocket, as
   a symbol of giving
   your prayer to God.

HOLY SPIRIT FIZZY PRAYERS

God has amazing power. In the Bible we see MIRACLES happening and the Holy Spirit transforming people's lives, changing them as they come to know how much God loves them. This prayer experiment is a very colourful way to ask the Holy Spirit to bring that amazing POWER into our lives and the lives of people we know.

YOU WILL NEED: Bicarbonate of soda, white vinegar, cups (3 or 4), food colouring (3 or 4 different colours), droppers or teaspoons, a baking tray or roasting tin.

1 Put some white vinegar into the three or four cups. Mix a different food colour into each cup of vinegar so that you end up with all different colours.

2 Cover the bottom of the baking tray or roasting tin with bicarbonate of soda.

3 Choose a colour of vinegar that represents yourself or someone you would like to pray for. Fill a dropper with some of that colour vinegar (or use a teaspoon).

4 Drop the vinegar on to the bicarbonate of
   soda and watch the explosion!

5 Pray that the Holy Spirit will come and
   transform the life of the person you have
   prayed for.

6 Repeat for another person with a different
   colour.

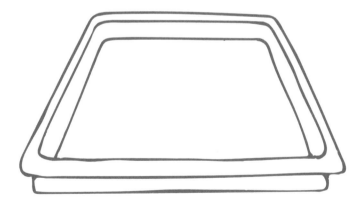